DOUBTF PASSENGER

Mastering the doubt in our mind and the world around us

(The omitted chapter from the book, Principles to Fortune)

Scott J. Bintz

Editing & assistance by Caleb Gwerder

This book may be purchased for educational, business or sales promotional use. For information, please email book@principlestofortune.com or visit www.principlestofortune.com

First published by Red Headed Rebel®
1618 Hwy 281 N
Jamestown, ND 58401
www.RedHeadedRebel.com

Dedicated to my mother, for always believing in me.

Want to Help Spread the Word About the Book?

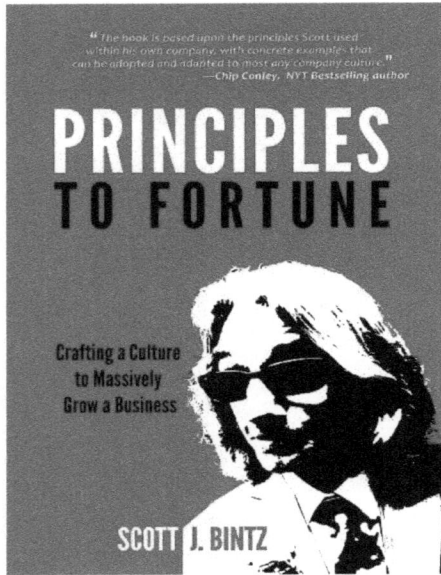

Visit: PrinciplesToFortune.com **& Sign Up:** To Our Newsletter

Share: Take a pic of the book, tag us and share it out

Hashtag: #PrinciplesToFortune

Connect Socially @

Facebook.com/principlestofortune/ - Instagram.com/principlestofortune

Snapchat.com/add/scottbintz - Linkedin.com/in/scottbintz

Twitter.com/bintzness101

Want an Autographed Copy?

Order online at PrinciplesToFortune.com

More About Scott: ScottBintz.com

PREFACE

"A hero is someone who, in spite of weakness,
doubt or not always knowing,
goes ahead and overcomes anyway"
-- Christopher Reeve

So after the book, Principles to Fortune, was published, I started getting interview and speaking requests. Some of these requests were about the contents of the book from entrepreneurship, work culture and e-commerce and others were more about the process of writing a book. When sharing on writing the book, I would say something like, "when writing the book, I had about 100,000 words of which, 60,000 or so were used in the book Principles to Fortune." There was a pretty large chapter titled, Doubtful Passenger, that was left out because it really didn't fit in with the context of the rest of the book. Then someone would ask, what was the chapter about? I would say it was about mastering or overcoming the doubt in one's mind and the world. Then they would ask, "will you publish it or can I get a copy." It's a pretty raw view of my mind and somewhat scary to kick out there. I originally wrote about this doubtful passenger, which is really my doubtful mind and the people out there in the world, that either slap a label on me or share why I can't do something. It's a gritty, rough and raw view of labels I've allow to be strapped to my mind from my inner self or other people, along with experiences and some insight to how I've improved or given context to these labels, which have freed and allowed me to do some pretty incredible things. One can't do something, if you don't first believe that possibly you can do it. A doubtful mind, will kill your passion, hopes and dreams if you allow it. The word mastering is used in describing this chapter, however that may suggest perfection. Look at it rather as a moving towards progress rather than an end destination. Also realize, limited editing has been done to this chapter. In any case, I hope you find it helpful. If you do, please let me know and pass it on to someone else it might be helpful to.

DOUBTFUL PASSENGER

"The mind is everything. What you think you become." -- Buddha

(This is the omitted chapter from the original publication of the book Principles To Fortune)

DNA – we are all unique. My goal is to be the best me I can be. Your goal should be the best you, you can be. None of us are great at everything. The "higher power" created us that way so we would need each other. This chapter is about my experience overcoming my doubtful mind. I hope some of my experience can help you along the way.

We all have a "doubtful passenger", it's in our mind and out in the world. It must be tamed with perspective. We seem to be born with it to some extent and the rest of it is nurtured and grown from our experience.

Mastering the doubtful passenger in one's mind, needs some self-discovery and perspective. There is also a doubtful passenger out in the world, that needs perspective and thoughtful interpretation. First let's go inside my mind; it's such a baffling place. My DNA is what it is. That's what I have to work with, I needed to discover what I'm good at and stop worrying about what I'm not good at.

Labels do not define anyone in absolute terms. Meaning 100% good/correct or 100% bad/incorrect, applies to no one. What are some of the labels you have strapped to your being? I say strapped because you believe them enough to attach them to your make up, your inner mind. The labels we allow be attached to us, are what fuels the doubtful passenger in our mind.

How many of them do you look at in absolute terms? They are generally not 100% right or 100% wrong. Do you look at them that way? Stop it. Change your perspective to look at them as percentages, not absolutes. Then do some real self-discovery. Are the labels you have attached to you accurate and if so to what extent? Once you know what they are and look at them more as a portion of the whole, then you can look to reduce them, enhance them or totally un-strap them from who you are. Some tuning and shifting may be in order. This doubtful passenger in my mind and yours, prevents us from taking action on our ideas and dreams. It must be tamed.

Here are some of the labels, I have been given over the years, some with and some without my blessing:

- Red Head
- Unnoticeable
- Buck-toothed Baby
- Bastard
- Carrot Top
- Red on the head, like a dick on a dog
- Tampon Head
- Skinny
- Tooth Pick
- Trouble Maker
- Kibbles n Bits
- Poor
- Rich
- Whiner
- Rule Breaker
- 2nd Class Guy

- Quitter

- Loser

- Never Gives Up

- Instigator

- Helpful

- Rebel

- Determined

- Crafty

- Weak

- Hot Tempered

- New Kid

- Stubborn

- Slow Reader

- Math Wizard

- Lazy

- Hard Worker

- Doesn't Follow Well

- Genius

- Dumb Ass

- Brilliant

- Asshole

- Bully

- Push Over

- Considerate

- Visionary

- Passionate

- Boring

- Introvert

- Extrovert

- Persistent

- Inspirational

- Insightful

- Close minded

- Open minded

- Teachable

- Unteachable

- Poor white trash

- Thoughtful

- Marketer

- Unqualified

- Reckless

- Cocky

- Lucky

- Defiant

- Inspiring

- Idiot

- Funny

- Not Funny

- Giving

- Wonderful

- Undisciplined

- Disciplined

- Underrated

- Overrated

- Out of My League

- Futurist

It's clear some of these labels are complete opposites. Some of them I naturally lean towards others creep up in little moments. Clearly this doesn't look like the same person when they are are together, but it is. All of them have degrees of truth.

If I think about one or two they become all encompassing almost like absolutes, but they are not. They are sections of a pie, a pie that has lots of layers, and many kinds of sprinkles on top. Key realization here is that none of these are always or never. They are tiny ingredients that make up the whole pie. Some of the sprinkles just apply a few times in a lifetime, some very good, some not so much. And others apply almost daily, but not any of them always. We have blessings to share and curses to bear.

I needed to accept who I was from my DNA, my experience, the good of me and the not so good. I need to turn my attention to the things I am good at or come naturally to me and enhance them. There is more gain and enjoyment to be had here. I need to rarely pay attention to the negative things that are moments or that I am bad at. The bad is where I need guidance and insight from others and for the things I am not good at, I need to let others do for me. If I suck at something and really want to get better at it, I should put some time and energy into it, seek counsel and practice. However, I need to have the awareness that this isn't something I'll probably ever be the best at or even sometimes mediocre. Rather, I need to learn to accept that being better than expected at something, is the reward.

When I was 9 or 10 years old, Pac-Mac came out. There was a video game machine two blocks from our trailer at the local grocery store, another one at El Roy's Pizza in the town east of us, and another one at the local video arcade in the town west of us. Why do I know this? Well... I was the first kid in the area to "turn it over", meaning going over 999,990 points and starting back at zero. How did a 10 year old figure this out? Not sure exactly, but somehow, I figured out it was a pattern. Once you figured out the pattern to gobble up the dots, you just repeated the pattern at every level. As long as you didn't mess up the exact path you needed to gobble up the dots, you could literally play for hours on one quarter.

That was good living for a young kid. I don't know how I learned the pattern. I just figured it out through trial and error. My trial and error was just "faster" than most. I would write out the pattern for other kids, most would have trouble sticking to it. They also would get pretty pissed that I was holding the game hostage. The store, pizza place and local arcade would unplug the game on me at closing time.

Kids would ask me how I figured it out, but I really struggled with explaining it to them. I'm guessing my response was that of a cocky, 9-year-old, who just whipped Pac-Man's ass, and it was something along the lines of, "I'm just smarter than you ha ha ha". I didn't realize at the time, that I was good at seeing certain patterns, especially patterns on how something works. Shortly after, the video game Defender came out, I sucked at that and wasn't sure why. It was a game I dropped many rolls of quarters into and never really got it mastered. This Pac-Mac pattern-seeing "DNA" skill would come in handy years later for search engine optimization on websites. That was also something that was hard for me to explain to others. But guess what, I down played the Pac-Man skill at the time. It was a fluke and I got lucky. But it was enjoyable to be "big man on campus" when near the Pac-Man machine.

Around that same time, I was involved in sports like baseball, soccer, football and basketball. I was a left hander with no father to show me how to play sports, without the awareness that you have to practice outside of practice if you really want to get good at something. Needless to say, I generally sucked at sports, but all my inner attention was focused on that. That is what I wanted to be good at. Playing sports badly is also where one can add to their doubtful passenger label collection.

Another event happened in 1980, Ernő Rubik, licensed his work to Ideal Toy Corp. It was invented in 1973, but once Ideal Toy Corp got ahold of it, it was highly marketed and made its way to our tiny trailer. I couldn't put it down. In short order, I discovered if you turned it, you could pop out one of the center pieces on the edge, take it apart and reassemble it completely. I took that bad boy to school, claiming to have solved it. Once a fellow classmate scrambled it, I thought I was doomed. After school, Rubik's Cube and I bonded after a long afternoon and evening. Somehow, I figured out it was a pattern. A couple combinations to solve it. It was originally advertised as having "over 3,000,000,000 (three billion) combinations", but only one solution. Good thing I didn't know this at the time, as I would have alienated myself and had no buddies. That information may have also prevented me from even trying to solve it, given the likelihood of this skinny, not very coordinated, redhead finding the 1 solution in 3 billion.

The next cool thing, once you knew the pattern to solve it, was to solve it in as few moves as possible. That competition at the time was a lonely one. As most kids my age had better things to do than learn how to solve it. When I would show kids and even some adults the pattern, it seemed most had a hard time remembering it unless I stood next to them and coached them virtually the entire way.

Since I didn't have any competitors to play for time or moves I quickly returned to focusing on things I wasn't very good at like following rules that made no sense and taking un-normal risks. Both taking risks and not following rules at the time were things that were hammered into me by authority figures as bad qualities, but I couldn't seem to shake them very well as a young kid. I just thought maybe there was something wrong with me or perhaps I was dumb or something.

When I was 12, I won a dirt bike playing pool. Don't get me wrong, I'm not good at pool, I just got lucky and was betting more than I had, but figured I had nothing to lose. I was correct that I didn't have anything of material value to lose. However, I did have something else to lose, but didn't realize it at the time. I would have lost my reputation for keeping my word or gotten myself into a real deep hole that I couldn't dig out of, had I lost. I thought winning the bike at the time was pretty cool, but it was quickly pushed aside by feeling bad for taking such a risk and by some unwritten rule you shouldn't "gamble" for such high stakes at my age. At the time, I thought it was a calculated risk given my pool skill vs an adult who had been drinking. It didn't seem like a risk and it didn't seem like breaking rules. Just seemed like it was time to win a dirt bike from someone who shouldn't be betting while intoxicated. After I got the dirt bike home, I was happy my Mom had gotten a six-foot tall fenced-in backyard for our dog, which was now a good safe storage area for my new prized possession. It wasn't a garage, but it would work for the time.

You couldn't ride a dirt bike in town, so I would have to push it to the edge of town and then ride it. That seemed like a bad rule/law so I found a work-around. I would put both hands on the handlebars, with both legs to the left of the dirt bike, which was running, then when no one was looking, I would softly sit with my right butt cheek on the seat and ride it. If I saw a car or person I would return to looking like I was pushing it. That, it seemed, was a better way to get a little more riding time in, rather than spend ½ of my free time pushing the bike out of town and then back home again.

When I was caught, I would be reprimanded. I would pay the imposed consequences, which normally included no riding dirt bike for a time and then resume my side saddling out of town. It seemed like I was still getting more riding time by side saddling the bike out of town and getting some consequences than I would have had with pushing the bike and no consequences.

Often, when the opportunity presented itself, I would let my buddies ride my dirt bike. Sometimes it was more rewarding and enjoyable watching them have a blast on the bike and benefiting from the opportunity. If the bike got damaged a bit, I was told kids were taking advantage of me. Nonetheless, I couldn't stop continuing the practice of letting others experience what I got to experience.

Going back to my youth, seeing patterns, risk taking, rule flexing for a good cause, improvising and considerateness are just inner drivers that are a part of my basic make up. At the time I thought I was like the labels that others gave to me: 100% weird, too risky, rule breaker, clever and taken advantage of. Clearly nothing there was 100% true all the time.

All of these labels created the doubtful passenger in my mind. When something is difficult, it's easy to grab a label, slap it on that problem or experience to re-enforce why I can't do something. Realizing these labels are never 100% and that I needed to change the label slapping process and use the ones that reinforce why I can do something. I need to look at these differently. Process them differently. Tune and shift them.

While in college in 1991, during the time you could walk into almost any gas station and grab a free cup of coffee, I pitched the idea of setting up a coffee shop in the student union and letting the business students run it. It would be good to make a few bucks, learn how to run a business and start it with a fairly low cost with a pile of customers walking by daily, all of which probably could use more caffeine. At the student union meeting after my pitch, a fellow student, said it was a ridiculous and crazy idea. I was shocked at his fairly harsh remarks. Seemed like the rest of the feedback by others was devoted to sharing why it wouldn't work and trying to troubleshoot who would manage it and how we would get the staff, which seemed like easy answers to me, once we decided to do it. I left, went back home and pondered. I grabbed my trusty labels of crazy and dumb slapped them on the experience and moved on. In hindsight, I have learned I should slap the label of persistence on it along with a dose of calculated risks and suggest "what's the worst that could happen?". And in business, I've learned sometimes listening to others only serves the value of getting insight how hard something is to do or why one shouldn't do it.

Like all new ideas, rarely are they accepted out of the gate. Sometimes one might "re-package" the idea and try again. Sometimes, it's just not the right time or even too soon. My doubtful passenger won. I just grabbed the wrong labels. Had I grabbed the right ones, my passenger would have been the hopeful and optimistic spirited one. I'm not suggesting the coffee shop idea would have panned out, rather my doubtful passenger killed it and I will never know.

During my last semester in college, landed a job with Western Wireless aka CellularONE. Cell towers were going up around the state and Minot was next on the list. Cell towers would be up three months after I was hired. We had a sales goal of eight phones a month. I was a bit taken aback. How the hell are we going to sell eight phones a month with no cell service? This was when the cost was $300 bucks for a brick phone and the service was $40 bucks a month per 30 minutes, plus long distance calling. On top of that, if you were roaming in a different town, a $3 access charge. My manager Carol, previously a 20-year veteran of landline phone service selling, said we could do it. I grabbed the labels desperation, 2nd class guy, risk and Carol's inspiration and went to work. Desperate was easy, because I needed a job to pay for the stacking bills and student loans. I worked hard, partly because of fear of failing and partly because I was worried Carol would realize she hired a 2nd class guy who couldn't hang with the big league.

During this time, I would attend class when I could, trying to finish my degree and then work on selling phones. My trusty label of lazy almost got me killed. With class, finals and work, I was exhausted day and night. I would drag myself out of bed and have to fight hard to stay motivated all day long. I made it through finals and was ready to graduate as I was looking forward to only work with no classes on the side. This tired and exhausted feeling continued when I was "only working". Finally a friend, suggested I go to the doctor. Turned out I had mono not laziness; which when you have mono and push yourself too hard, it makes you feel worse. Thank goodness for friends.

Realize, the label in my mind as being described as lazy could have gotten me killed. To my surprise, we hit our goals. I learned other people's belief and inspiration can get you going and that the passion I had for being a part of an emerging technology quickly replaced desperation. The label of desperations began to shift into futurist (my meaning is embracing technology early). Having the label, 2nd class guy and underrated, probably came in handy because feeling that way made my sales pitches for why one should by a phone were factual in nature and tamed with why it would help. This led to a promotion to another market to be the manager. Holy balls, I couldn't believe I was picked. I felt there were better people for the job, at least from the perspective of comparing my inner raw labels and feelings about myself to other peoples' outward appearances. This again was me picking a few labels like not smart enough and dumb luck and seeing them as dominate, rather than the whole picture. Later I learned I received the management job because she felt I was teachable and a hard worker, which clearly are opposite of the dumb and lazy labels. The trip to the doctor told me that some labels are just wrong or out of context.

On to a new market. With some luck I got an office set up using only 50% of the budget, hired a friend to be a salesperson for me and started working on developing the new market. We needed to recruit some authorized dealers and go after business users directly. Most of the time I felt like they are going to find out I don't know what I'm doing. From the inside it looked like I was learning by the seat of my pants, doing everything last minute and at some point someone - a customer, my boss, an authorized dealer or my staff - was going to point out poor white trash was unqualified and shouldn't be managing things. Those things kept me learning, thinking and pushed me to be more creative. In retrospect, I don't think most folks saw me this way. Based on feedback I later learned, most saw me as hard working, passionate, smart yet a little socially awkward.

We started running funny ads on the radio about the character named "Will Call More", which I paid for out of my pocket to help the cause. We got three authorized dealers going and started pitching groups of people rather than one on one. Sometimes we would pitch to thirty realtors, and maybe one would buy a phone. At the time we had bag phones, brick style phones and the new Motorola flip phone. I would end my pitch with throwing the phone on the ground to demonstrate how strong it was, each time hoping this wasn't the time it would break. My calculated risk taking of throwing a phone on the floor certainly helped with closing sales.

We were selling phones left and right and received permission to hire an office manager and a second sales person. We were paid a base salary and then had a monthly commission and quarterly bonus program. I learned then, if you ever want to know a loophole in a commission or bonus structure, just ask the salesperson on it. Quickly, I realized you could make more money selling zero phones one month and forty the next rather than twenty each month. Also, for the quarterly bonus that included all phones sold by us and our authorized dealers. For the last quarter of the year, I wanted to really kill it. I did some math and figured out if we discounted the phones, even out of our own pocket, and sold a certain amount of phones on two-year plans instead of one-year plans, we would make three to five times more commission plus the bonus on top.

We bought down the cost of the phones at $100 each for the quarter, out of our own pockets, for a 2 year service plan. The money to be made was in the service plan, but the customer needed a phone for the service. If we made the phone cheaper, more people would buy them and in order to buy a phone they had to sign up for the cell service. It helped the customer get into a phone for less money, it helped us make money and it helped the company get longer agreements. My boss thought the idea was genius and we launched it advertising phones at $100 off.

The result, we sold more phones in our market than anywhere else in the state. We exploded the commission and bonus structure. I won a trip to Bellevue,

WA and a peak achievement award from the company and the commissions and bonus were crazy big.

Two months later, the company totally redesigned the commission and bonus structure. I was demoted back to an account executive for running an unauthorized promotion. My boss, Carol, denied she gave me permission to run the phone discount program to the regional manager. I was a crafty rule breaker who got lucky. I was shocked she could look me in the eye and tell me she did not give me permission. I got the label as a rule breaker, even though, technically I didn't break a rule, I got permission, the idea was solid, it was a game changer and it worked.

As you probably know, this is a common practice today to discount the price of the phone if you get the cell service, but at the time it was not. My ego couldn't handle the demotion at the time, so I began looking for a new job. I felt this 2nd class guy wouldn't fit in with the corporate world. I also felt that I couldn't be cold and calculating with people in the corporate world like what I experienced. However, I left with a few more wanted labels like rule breaker for a good cause, genius, crafty and calculated risks aren't bad. Lucky rather than good. I'll take it.

I still looked at these labels way to much as all or nothing. However, I also began to see that just because someone says something, coesn't make it so and that some labels can be shifted or flexed into another. As for Carol, I could understand why she threw me under the bus. She was in her 40's, wanted to take care of her family, probably didn't want to be looking for a new job and demoting me was easier for her to do than speaking the truth.

Carol was an honest person, yet at work with the fear of losing her job, she ignored her own values. Fairly quickly I didn't have any ill will toward Carol. A good friend, helped me be open minded and to see it from her point of view which prevented any resentment from growing.

I also realized making a bunch of money didn't really change the way I looked at myself. It felt super sweet to see a big commission check, but was soon replaced with feeling bad after I spent it too fast. Plus, it felt like making money was the main goal in that environment, rather than being useful or helpful. I wanted to do something that felt like it was more about being helpful than making money for the sake of making money.

Often, I've been given the label of marketer or sometimes great marketer. In reality, I'm not a marketer, more of a promoter. Meaning, I was good at getting the word out to the masses, whatever that word may be. Whether by lots and lots of phone calls, faxes and over time emails, social posts and so forth.

So I started letting people I know, personally and professionally, that I was looking for another job. Milt of Nitsche Communications, one of the authorized cellular dealers we had set up, told me two brothers in a town north of us, were making pickup covers and farm tarps and they were looking for a sales rep. This was the spring of 1994. I didn't know it then, but this would change the course of my business life.

I got an interview, jumped into my Honda Accord and wheeled it to Courtenay, ND. This is where I first met Chuck and Steve Schmeichel, two brothers that owned Agri-Cover, Inc., which at the time made about a million or so in business, mainly selling roll tarps for farm trucks.

The interview was with Chuck. He asked me if I had any experience setting up dealers. He was looking for someone to set up dealers for his pickup covers and farm covers around the country. I shared my experience with setting up a few cellular dealers.

He got a phone call. After the call, he asked me if I was in Winnipeg at a trade show and couldn't find a hotel room, what would I do? I said, I'd keep calling hotels and work my way out. Probably call the nicer hotels and see if they know of any hotels with rooms. He asked, so you wouldn't call me? I said why would I call you, you have better things to be doing and probably wouldn't have any leads on hotel rooms in Winnipeg. He said "good" and "your hired." Turned out, the salesman he had just called, was up in Winnipeg and couldn't find a hotel room and was calling

Chuck for help. I said I would love the job, but would need a month to leave CellularONE.

This new job was for about ½ the pay as I was making at the time, even as an account executive without benefits except vacation pay. But something told me I could be more helpful there than at my current job and that Chuck could teach me a thing or two. A broken ego can produce some humility. Making a pile of money for just the sake of making money wasn't fulfilling.

Somewhere I knew that the value and learning one gains from an experience can be unmeasurable, it is often greater than the actual pay. Opportunity and experience are greater than any amount of "right-now" pay. This was a huge risk, but I never looked at it that way. It looked like an opportunity; and boy it was. Risk taker and rebel are labels others give me. To me they look like opportunity and like there has to be a better way to do something.

Since I was trying to get back to the business of being useful, I looked at my new role as an opportunity to help those at the company. When I set up dealers, that helped the company be profitable, which in turn would mean the company could better take care of its people. I didn't know anything about this business, so I asked a lot of questions.

Since I had the ear of the owners, I used my promotion skills to urge them to set up a 401k and health insurance for the employees. The repackage and try again philosophy was at work here. Chuck always paid folks very well and figured they would save their own money and get their own insurance. I was steadfast that employees didn't look at it this way. People naturally look at what they don't have rather than what they do have.

When I started out in life, I didn't have too many connections, but I did have a lot of persistence; an insane amount for some reason. This persistence makes for being a good promoter. If you don't succeed, try again, re-package, re-invent. It also got me in some jams, but open mindedness along with persistence makes for some creative ideas and solutions.

Chuck ultimately agreed, since I was a persistent SOB, provided he didn't have to set it up. So over time employees got those benefits and more. The accounting manager along with the owners got the credit for this. Feeling underrated and undeserving at times were really assets to help keep my ego in check. No one really looked at me as a threat per say. It didn't matter to me who got the credit, what mattered was the result. Feeling like a 2nd class guy and driven by a spirit of being helpful makes for faster results when I'm not delayed by thinking for some reason that I need to get the credit. The saying 'there is no limit to how far you can go, if you don't care who gets the credit' seemed to have some merit. I also gladly accepted insane "persistence" as part of my core make up. Something to be embraced and accepted for its good and sometimes not so good.

I thought, if I was going to be selling pickup covers, I better get a pickup. I got a 1994 Dodge Ram. Showed it to Chuck, he pointed out it was a long bed and a two wheel drive. Long beds are good for work, but not so good for demonstrating a cover and a two wheel drive in North Dakota is not very smart. I should have sought counsel.

Good news is my labels were getting tuned. In this case, I realized I was dumb, but just for a moment, at buying pickups and learned when you don't know about something, go to an expert to speed up the learning curve. I would often think about this as I drove the truck for the next few years, especially on the snow days I would be in the ditch waiting to get towed out by someone with a four wheel drive truck. Sometimes good character is made by riding out one's bad decisions. That truck helped set up a lot of new dealers from Washington to Indiana.

I was very grateful and began to realize, the dumb label strapped to me was now somewhat limited and could be prevented or reduced by asking for help and being open minded. And to have success not everything has to be perfect. Sometimes you just have to do the best with what you have, rather than use what you have or don't have, as an excuse for not doing something. Good at improvising,

I'll take it. I rather liked that label.

I was mainly focused on marketing and setting up dealers for the pickup cover. The philosophy at the time was you had to "show it to sell it". This was done by attending trade shows and calling on potential dealers. We also hired some other salespeople. Everyone seemed to have their own style. Some were good with accounts we already had, some were good at finding new accounts, some were good at working trade shows and others better at marketing. I fell into the "good" at finding new accounts and marketing.

Even in this area, people had their own styles. I was more of a prospector. Others were more calculated. Meaning, I figured out that if I called on eight potential dealers a day, I would set one up. Others would call on one to four bigger dealers in a week and maybe land a really big one every other week or so. I felt my system was better, more reliable and more effective. But trying to get the others to follow suit was nearly impossible. Personalities, skills and leanings were all very different. There were things we were each clearly bad at and others we were really good at. Each had their place. Each were needed at various times. Everyone got their share of labels slapped on them.

The real awareness was that people all contributed, but in different ways. When we had to entertain bigger accounts, the more fun sales reps were great at this. When we had to discuss business, the more creative and calculated reps were great at this. If we just did my system, we would only have small dealers, but since we embraced everyone's styles we had small, medium and very large accounts. This was good for keeping business balanced as well.

What I'm getting at is this; when we look at someone, we look at them and judge them for how we would do their job or their role if we were in it. Sometimes we do this without considering a few more things that are really important like, their unique make up, skills and experience along with all of ours in that same role or job.

For example, a customer service manager might be really great at creating fun and excitement for the team, but not so good at administering employee discipline. So it's easy for me to judge, slap a label on the person and say, this person sucks at discipline and if I was the CS manager, I'd be better at discipline. Which may be the case, but I'm not considering what I wouldn't be so good at, like perhaps creating fun and excitement for the CS team. Employee disciple might be really strong, but we might not have any employees to disciple if there isn't some fun and excitement going on.

In this case, if I'm the CS manager's boss, I should realize that this person could get some training and perhaps get a little better at it, but a better solution might be to get him or her someone else to help with the discipline so she or he can focus on creating more fun and excitement for employees and customers. They are good at it already, so do more of that. I've learned you will give way to the best results from doing more of what you are good at and less of what you are not. If I'm the employee, I should have the awareness that my boss can't be the best at everything and I should try to help them in areas I'm strong.

This would be a key ingredient in helping me understand my strengths and weaknesses and understanding them in others. At RealTruck, this perspective would help employees and managers not expect everyone to be great at everything. The awareness that everyone can't be great at everything, is very valuable. This, I think, was why the managers at RealTruck really excelled, because they didn't expect that we were great at everything. We just encouraged them to do more of what they were good at and ask for help on those things they were not.

Once RealTruck was going, my labels were expanding, some good and some not so good. It became really apparent when one day, I was getting an award for innovation and described as a genius and early in the day, being described as a rude dumb ass by an employee because I jumped to conclusions and lectured a web developer about why details are important and how a failed development publish was hurting the company. Had I started with questions rather than assumptions, I would have found out it was a third party that dropped the ball and the developer had worked all night to fix the issue and was going to stay on it until we got it right.

It was an emotional roller coaster. These labels seemed to be absolutes in my mind, swinging daily from one extreme to another. I had to learn how to get them into perspective, for my sake and for the sake of those around me. It's really hard to accept an award for innovation, when you are feeling like a rude asshole who should be smart enough to ask questions.

On the drive home I thought about all the labels, why they echoed in my head, why I let them define me. How could I enhance the ones I liked and get rid of the ones I didn't like or want? I pondered. My head hurt thinking about it. My mind raced all night and it felt like I didn't get much sleep.

Driving into the office, I thought about how I could feel dumb and like a genius all on the same day, hours apart from each other, almost an all encompassing feeling. It's struck me these are brief moments and not infinite. In my head these feelings and labels seem to either create self-doubt or cockiness. Really, what I would like to have is more self-awareness and realistic confidence. Those seemed more attractive to have rather than overwhelming doubt or a fake confidence, disguised as cockiness.

I got to my office. Earlier in life a friend had taught me about taking a personal inventory. To take a look at the good things and the bad things. I decided I would write an inventory on all the labels I tended to apply to myself. You would have read it earlier in this chapter.

I looked at it. First, it was apparent that the list was full of conflicts. Second, was many of them only applied for a moment in time. Which ones really applied to me? Which ones applied on a regular basis? Those seemed to be the important ones. Some I liked and some I didn't. The ones that seemed to be regular that I didn't like, maybe I needed to accept that about myself or learn a way to change it. When I looked back at some of the things I overcame in my life, like these labels, the ones I liked, that were more dominate, seemed to be the very things that reduced my self-doubt enough to move forward. Holy batman, this awareness was huge.

This would be the awareness I needed to look at myself and others differently moving forward. No one including myself was 100% anything. Turns out, some of the labels simply didn't apply at all really. Who I really am and who I really want to be was right there in black and white. I would keep my dominate labels, at least the ones I liked, handy. When I had self-doubt, I would look at it. This process seemed to help me make decisions easier. It also gave me the awareness to ask for help on things other people were good at that I was not.

Here is the process I went through to reduce my self-doubt:

Inventory

1. Write a list of all the labels your mind tells you that you have.

2. Highlight in green, the ones that apply to you most of time.

3. Highlight in yellow, the ones that rarely apply.

4. Circle the ones you like.

5. Mark an X next to the ones you don't like.

Realization

1. The green highlighted labels are your dominate ones.

2. The yellow highlighted labels are moments in time to be learned from.

3. The ones highlighted green, that you like, are the ones to use to support why you can do something.

4. The ones highlighted green that you don't like, are the ones you need to accept or find a way to improve and ask others for help.

5. The ones you like or don't like that are highlighted yellow or not highlighted at all are minor to who you really are. They are just moments.

Share and Feedback

1. Bring your list to a very close friend and let them know you want honest feedback.

2. Share it with them and ask if your realizations are accurate.

3. Adjust your list as needed. Your friend may have some perceptions you cannot see.

Actions

1. Keep your green highlighted list you like handy, that is to be referred to whenever you have self-doubt as to why you can do something.

2. Realize no one thing, one experience or one day defines who you are or who other people are.

3. When you have trouble, ask for candid feedback from a trusted friend. Trust their judgement of your situation as it is probably more accurate than yours, as they are not emotionally involved in the situation.

4. Keep learning however you can. Make time for it. Learning is the spark for doing.

Moving forward with this new awareness helped transform me into a better leader. To focus more on what I'm good at and empower others around me to do the same rather than focus on why I or someone else is not good at.

Persistence and determination are good traits to have. I wish you much of both of those traits along with much luck with taming your personal doubtful passenger and even kicking its' ass from time to time. Smile and pass it on.

Want to Help Spread the Word About the Book?

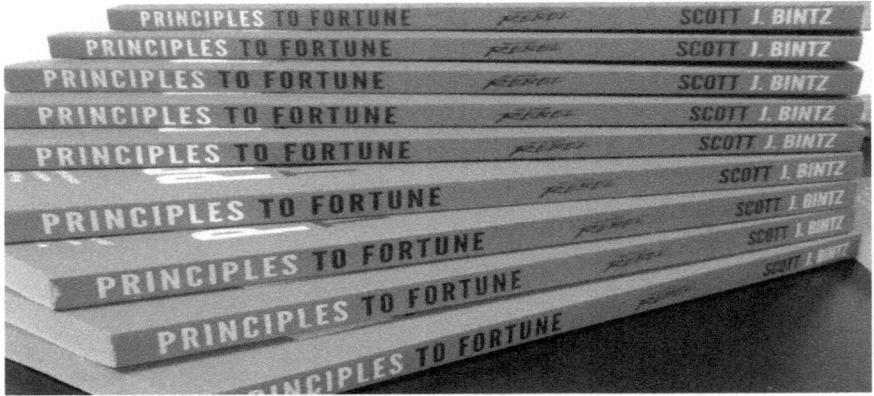

Visit: PrinciplesToFortune.com **& Sign Up:** To Our Newsletter

Share: Take a pic of the book, tag us and share it out

Hashtag: #PrinciplesToFortune

Connect Socially @

Facebook.com/principlestofortune/ - Instagram.com/principlestofortune

Snapchat.com/add/scottbintz - Linkedin.com/in/scottbintz

Twitter.com/bintzness101

Want an Autographed Copy?

Order online at PrinciplesToFortune.com

More About Scott: ScottBintz.com

www.ingramcontent.com/pod-product-compliance
Lightning Source LLC
Chambersburg PA
CBHW022100210326
41520CB00046B/794